Grown-Up Children, Grown-Up Parents